Computers

... and stuff!

by

Owen Jones

Copyright

Published by:
Megan Publishing Services
https://meganthemisconception.com

Copyright Owen Jones 2024 ©

Computers

Hello and thank you for your interest in this ebook called 'Computers'.

Step into the captivating world of Computers ...and stuff! a not-very-technical exploration of computers and peripherals. In this book, we'll take a pragmatic look at how computers have evolved, and impacted our lives today.

Forty years ago, very, very few members of the public were interested in computes. Even twenty years ago, many people of all ages knew little about them, but look around you now!

Computers invites readers of all backgrounds to appreciate the transformative power of technology and consider the possibilities that lie ahead. Together, let's embark on this illuminating voyage to better understand the ever-changing world of computing.

I hope that you will find the information helpful, useful and profitable.

The information in this ebook on various aspects of computers, peripherals and related subjects is organized into 21 chapters of about 500-600 words each.

I hope that it will interest those who are interested in computers, the Internet, peripherals, electronics and using them in a practical fashion.

As an added bonus, I am granting you permission to use the content on your own website or in your own blogs and newsletter, although it is better if you rewrite them in your own words first.

If you have any feedback, please leave it with the company you bought this book.

Regards,
Owen Jones

Table of Contents

Dere V14 Air Notebook – A Review

This article is my own personal experience with the Dere V14 Air Notebook, which I bought a little while ago. I will not be going into all the specifications of this device, because you can find this information on the manufacturer's website. I will say that it comes with Windows 10 Pro and the Intel core i7 processor though.

My first impression was that it is small and came with unadvertised accessories. I have been using 17 inch laptops for a decade, and didn't realise how much smaller 14 inches is. That is my fault. I should have done. However, it becomes a real problem when you transfer your spreadsheets across. If they were made to make full use of the larger screen, then there will be data that is not visible without scrolling, and if you resize the spreadsheet, the data will appear very small. You may need (stronger) glasses!

It is very light, but that was not a reason why I bought this device anyway.

The screen shows very vivid colours. It is the best screen I have ever worked with without a shadow of a doubt. It is very easy on the eyes. The sound capabilities of the Dere V14 Air Notebook are, however, not in the same league. I listen to the radio a lot when I am working, or not too, but I can often hardly hear it, which is completely unlike the Asus machines that I have been using for the last seven or eight years.

I will need to buy external speakers.

The Dere V14 Air laptop does not come with a carrying case, which I consider to be a serious fault. Why would a company that is proud of itself not provide a case with its name on it? In fact, this computer doesn't have its name on it at all.

That is just weird!

And another strange thing is the camera. It is on the hinge with the screen. I don't know whether it is an Asian/Caucasian thing, but in normal work mode, the camera is focusing just above my head. I suppose that is why they give you a free external camera, which should be unnecessary.

Yet another 'free accessory' that should be unnecessary is the USB hub. This device has only ONE measly USB port in this day and age! I am sure that the original specifications stated two ports - one normal and one high-speed. I would never have bought a computer with just one.

The three best features of this $600 laptop are the screen, the Intel core i7 CPU and the solid-state drive (SSD). It is so fast! I didn't know what I was missing, and will never go back to spinning disks.

My feelings are mixed at the moment, but I think that I just about come down on the side of the Dere V14 Air Notebook.

*** Update: six months on, and the mouse pad has risen out of its well! Really! It has lost most of its functionality, and the batteries no longer hold any power at all.

I will never buy one of these again!

Owen Jones

Computer Hardware Training

In our modern world of hi-tech computers and fast networks, it is quite easy to become baffled about what you need to run a reasonable system. Many amateurs and professionals alike are constantly challenged by the new developments and innovations that are constantly taking place in the realms of computer casings, network adapters, monitors and the like.

Many people are frequently confronted with situations related to computers and the hardware. This is why computer hardware training is necessary for everyone who wants to either take the hobby seriously or treat it as a business. The basic knowledge and skills that you will acquire from proper computer hardware training will never go to waste.

Many modern companies around the country are eager to develop their businesses which would involve bigger networks and bigger IT departments. Modern businesses are either wholly handled by computers and servers or with the assistance of them. This means that if the IT department fails, then the whole company could come to a standstill or worse. They could even fail.

This is the reason why IT and hardware technicians are in such high demand. Technicians with advanced computer hardware training are pursued insistently by the big corporate giants who need the expertise of these skilled professionals. Huge benefits await these people at these companies and they are looked after very well.

For this reason many young people are now hoping to become computer and IT experts or technicians. There are various qualification levels in computer hardware training available from advanced specialization to basic computer hardware training courses.

But the challenge for any newcomer to this subject is the priceless experience that is gained from the field of operations. However, before all that can happen you should make sure that your training is conducted at a recognized centre in IT.

There are many fraudsters and cheats operating freely around the country and so it is best to be careful when you are choosing your computer hardware training course.

A search for the best computer hardware training centres online would be the easiest way to go about looking for a good technical centre Most of these centres are certified by the pertinent authorities and the proper identification can be made when you visit their individual websites.

When the summer holidays start to get near, many parents begin to look for chances for their children to gain more experience and ability. An answer to this problem could be a summer camp that provides computer hardware training and IT training. These computer camps would definitely bring a definite advantage to these youngsters when they eventually have to go out into the adult world.

So, if this is the direction you want to go in, stop worrying about it and get on with working towards joining a computer hardware training course as soon as you can. Take advantage of the chances available to you and begin to plan your life. Look into getting yourself some computer hardware training today, right now!

Common Computer Viruses

New computer viruses are being generated, exposed and fought every day. These computer viruses are created often just to annoy us and to wreak mayhem in our computer systems. Hereunder, I have described ten viruses currently cited as being the most widespread and being potentially able to inflict the most destruction.

However, new viruses are being developed daily, so this list is by no means complete. The best thing you can do is remain alert, keep your anti-virus software updated, and keep aware of the current computer virus threats.

Virus: Trojan.Lodear:
A Trojan (from Trojan Horse) that tries to download files from a remote source. It will inject a .dll file into the EXPLORER.EXE process causing system instability.

Virus: W32.Beagle.CO@mm:
A mass-mailing worm that lowers security settings. It can delete security-related registry sub keys and may prevent admittance to security-related websites.

Virus: Backdoor.Zagaban:
A Trojan that permits the compromised computer to be operated as a covert proxy and which may decrease network performance.

Virus: W32/Netsky-P:
A mass-mailing worm which propagates by emailing itself to addresses produced from files on the local drives.

Virus: W32/Mytob-GH:
A mass-mailing worm and IRC backdoor Trojan for the Windows platform. Messages sent by this worm will have the subject chosen randomly from a list including titles such as: Notice of account limitation, Email Account Suspension, Security measures,   Members   Support,   Important Notification.

Virus: W32/Mytob-EX:

A mass-mailing worm and IRC backdoor Trojan similar in nature to W32-Mytob-GH. W32/Mytob-EX runs constantly in the background, providing a backdoor server which allows a distant hacker to gain access and control over your computer via IRC channels. This virus spreads by sending itself to email attachments harvested from your email address book.

Virus: W32/Mytob-AS, Mytob-BE, Mytob-C, and Mytob-ER:
This family of worm variations has similar characteristics in terms of what they can do. They are mass-mailing worms with backdoor functionality that can be controlled through the Internet Relay Chat (IRC) network.   Additionally, they can propagate themselves via email and through various operating system vulnerabilities such as the LSASS (MS04-011).

Virus: Zafi-D:
A mass-mailing worm and a peer-to-peer worm which replicates itself to the Windows system folder with the filename Norton Update.exe. It can then generate a quantity of files in the Windows system folder with filenames consisting of 8 random characters and a DLL extension. W32/Zafi-D

replicates itself to folders with names containing words like 'share', 'upload', or 'music' as 'ICQ 2005a new!.exe' or 'winamp 5.7 new!.exe'. W32/Zafi-D will also display a fake error message box with the caption "CRC: 04F6Bh" and the text "Error in packed file!".

Virus: W32/Netsky-D:
A mass-mailing worm with IRC backdoor functionality which can also infect computers vulnerable to the LSASS (MS04-011) exploit.

Virus: W32/Zafi-B:
A peer-to-peer (P2P) and email worm that will reproduce itself to the Windows system folder as a randomly named EXE file. This worm will test for the presence of an Internet connection by trying to connect to google.com or microsoft.com. A bilingual, worm with an attached Hungarian political text message box which translates to "We demand that the government accommodates the homeless, tightens up the penal code and VOTES FOR THE DEATH PENALTY to cut down the increasing crime. Jun. 2004, SNAF Team"

Computer Repair Training

You frequently hear someone say that computers are taking over the world and it is indubitably true that a personal computer is a must for any enterprising individual hoping to establish him or her self in the world. The Internet and the personal computer have revolutionized the world in so many ways that it is it involved in almost all business activity these days.

Because of this, computer repair training is a thriving industry too. It is also practical to have some computer repair training oneself. For what would you do, if your personal computer; with all your valuable data, breaks down on a Sunday morning when all the computer repair shops are shut?

This is why some computer repair training is very important for all professionals and students hoping for ways to break through to the top. For them, computer repair skills would be a definite benefit.

Information Professionals across the world realize that it is necessary to obtain computer repair training. But avoiding computer repair training is a common error committed by young executives. The basic computer knowledge gained by computer repair training is essential when you are in a difficult situation. Some executives have understood the advantage of becoming certified by computer repair training centres.

But aside from executives becoming certified, many young people aspire to become professional computer technicians. It is certainly essential for young technicians to acquire suitable computer repair training from recognized institutes or universities. There are some companies that can deceive you into becoming certified by an inferior education establishment. This is most common on the Internet.

Although computer repairing seems like a low grade job, most people overlook the important fact that a high level of demand is being created by businesses and technology driven companies that need certified and experienced technicians to help run their business.

Therefore these technicians are well sought after. Although the fact remains that some technicians get fooled by phony colleges and get into bother when they begin working for real.

The correct selection of a computer repair training centre is therefore essential for young enthusiasts looking for a good job.

There are various levels of computer repair training on hand, from fundamental training to specialization in specific areas of computer repair and technological know-how. The basic training is targeted at professionals looking for some basic training to help them in their day to day commercial activities. The professional programs are available for IT Technicians who are looking for advanced qualifications.

Therefore, do not squander any more time thinking about computers and the problems they can be and start looking for a proper computer repair training program at a recognized centre right away.

Owen Jones

Effective Ways To Start Blogging

Everybody has something to say and most people are passionate about something that they would like to talk on. Individuals would like to take this desire to talk a couple of stages further - they would like to tell the world about it. That was impossible less that twenty years ago, unless you managed to get on TV or were syndicated in the world's press. Now, obviously, anyone can do it.

The Internet makes it possible for everybody to have their say. The young and the old, the rich and the poor can discuss what they like on the Internet. You can use a website as your soap box or you could use a specialized web site called a blog. If you cannot have your own web site for any reason, you could open a free blog at one of the many web sites that offer free blogs.

The word 'blog' is short for 'web log' and adding an piece to your blog is known as blogging. Blogs have become a very effective means of spreading one's point of view. The latest form of blogging is micro-blogging, which is the generic description for Twitter.

Blogging has been used effectively by peoples of countries where the provision of human rights is not a government priority. Only recently, dissidents in Iran, Iraq and Myanmar have kept the world up-to-date about repression in their countries through blogs. The blogs were frequently reprinted in the world press and reported on the International news.

If you would like to blog for free, search Google for 'free blogs' and take a look about. There are dozens of free blog sites about and they all offer different features. Blogger by Google is one of the better ones, but there really are loads of different kinds of free blogs.

One thought is whether you would like your blog to be open or closed. That is, do you want anyone to be able to read it or do you want just a closed user group (CUG), which could include your friends, your family or your colleagues.

It ought to not take longer that thirty minutes to set up your blog. Some providers like to approve new blogs, but others do not. You could be blogging within the hour, so compose an piece welcoming people to your blog and post it to the blog. Make it 'sticky' if you can, so that it is always the first post that people read when they arrive at your blog.

Make your posts educational and endeavour to keep them topical. They should neither be so short that it is not worth coming to read them nor so long that they get boring - 400 to 500 is judged to be about correct.

You will have to advertise your blog or no-one will know that it is there. Do this by posting your pieces (with your blog address attached) to a few article directories. It is free and will give your blog a real boost in circulation. You can quit doing this when your blog is self-sustaining.

Allow all visitors to make comments on the blog, because it encourages them to come back, but check regularly for spam comments and delete them because a blog full of spam looks neglected.

Owen Jones

26

Clear Computer Case

What is a see-through computer casing and what can it do for you? Well, before we begin talking about the transparent computer case, allow me to inquire you something: what does your computer's case signify to you? I might even inquire: what does your computer signify to you? I ask this because your reply will ascertain what you want for your computer and its housing or casing.

Most people have always been happy enough with the simple, average light-grey housing that comes as bog-standard with the preponderance of computers. A number of have never even had a second thought about it. But at the same time there are others who have thought about their computer's case a lot and who yearn for something extraordinary for their computer.

A few of these individuals were accomplished at metalwork, others at woodwork and a few at glassware and there are a few truly fantastic, futuristic, home-produced housings out there. Particularly among the gaming community. However, we are not all so talented with our hands, but that does not signify that we have to be landed with a grey computer casing.

The easiest choice, if you want a designer computer housing is to construct one out of acrylic - the type of material used to build most fish tanks. You can buy and easily cut sheets of acrylic for the sides and stick them all together with acrylic resin. That may sound tricky, but it certainly is not.

Firstly you would have to research the architecture of a normal computer casing and then just reproduce it in acrylic. You might construct a see-through computer case in a weekend.

Or you might buy a clear computer housing kit. These kits arrive in flat-packs just like most kitchen fittings and can be easily assembled according to the instructions with a screwdriver. No cutting, no measuring, just a little gentle screwing.

And I mean gentle, as the screws that come with the see-through computer casing packs are usually made of acrylic too and will break easily. It is the only element of the construction procedure that calls for a cautionary note, because you don't want to have to drill out a shattered screw, do you? That would only put a dampener on your fun.

So why would anyone desire a see-through computer casing? I expect that there are many reasons. A few individuals may just want to be different and others may want to show that they can assemble or even build such a case. However, the translucent computer housing also has artistic and practical advantages. At least the good ones do.

On the Aesthetic Front: enthusiasts add neon lights and small LEDs that flash on and off or just glow eerily, maybe activated by some event, like a hard drive coming to life. These displays are called 'themes' and are normally red or blue, but can be almost any conceivable colour. Then you can include coloured fans (or paint your existing ones). You already have at least one fan in your case and probably two or three.

On the Practical Front: loads of people like to see what is going on inside their computer casing and it is neither practical nor safe to remove the cover all together. Additionally, creating your own clear computer case permits you to add more fans as over-heating is the main cause of hardware malfunction. The more fans the better.

A translucent computer housing would also allow you to see whether a fan has failed, which would result in over-heating in a standard casing and guaranteed hardware malfunction, whereas you would see it going on through your clear computer housing and replace the fan before crucial injury and loss of data might take place.

Computers For Kids

Anyone who has not been in a young children's classroom for thirty years or almost certainly even ten years may have a difficult time guessing, which age group the equipment is meant for. Kids nowadays are much more aware of what adults would call the 'adult world', because kids grow up so fast now that they are invading the adult world.

There are still lots of adults who are wary of computers, but not many children are that afraid by them. Children love the Internet and are not worried of using computers to access it. Older individuals have a reverence for computers that children have never picked up.

They are not in awe of them - there is no mystique surrounding computers for them. Computers are just standard items to them. Kids may not understand how they work, but hey! that's the case of most items as far as children are concerned.

This is perhaps something that parents ought to take into account whilst preparing their children for school or even kindergarten - not that children require a lot of encouragement to get on the Net. Most parents have more trouble keeping them off it!

Anyway, the fact is that many modern kindergartens have computers for the kids to get on line. This does not mean that the children are being forced to go on line, it is merely that there is a lot of educational material on line that teachers can use in these days of cut-backs on resources and kids and their parents expect to see a computer in the classroom as well.

It is worth talking to the school teacher and finding out what degree of computer knowledge is expected of kids going to that school. It will not be advanced, but it is worth making sure that they are up to that level, even if it is just so that they do not feel out of place in class.

The access that these school computers have to the Net will be fairly restricted, so there is no need to worry that the kids will be seeing inappropriate material and you should set up an 'account' or 'user profile' on your home computer that is similar to the one in school.

This is done by the use of programs known as 'net nannies'. You can also use the net nanny built into Windows and you can block individual web sites as well. Enquire of what system is in use at school and how it is configured. Copy that onto your home computer but only configure your children's account(s) with it.

This means that everyone in the household will have to log in at home: The kids will log in to an account with restricted access and the adults will log into an account or accounts with unlimited access. This is not difficult to set up.

This is not a fail-safe method of preventing older children from accessing unsuitable web sites, but it is all you will need for keeping young children safe, although parents should always show an interest in what their children are doing on line and they should alter their passwords frequently.

Owen Jones

34

Computer Cases

Is your computer's case or housing of any importance to you? You may be asking yourself the question: why should it be? The fact is that the computer case is important to the computer itself and also to some people.

Let's start with the computer's point of view. One, if not the key causes of computer failure is excessive heat. Which is why, when computers were first used in factories and large offices, the dedicated computer room was cut off from dust and was air conditioned, if not cooled especially. In those days, thirty-forty years ago, computer parts were very fragile and extremely expensive.

Nowadays, they are very, very much less expensive but they are still subject to bother from heat. Extreme heat will twist the boards, especially the motherboard because it is large, inside the computer case. They are not made for these gymnastics and sooner or later the very thin connections soldered onto the surface of the board will crack and inhibit the flow of electricity. It will die.

In order to prevent this happening, producers put fans inside the computer in order to boost the flow of air. There are usually at least two in a desktop computer case, one fitted in to the external casing and one directly on the CPU (the chip), which is often the hottest and most expensive single part. In laptops, where air flow is even more limited, there may be three or four fans.

So, these fans increase the circulation of air within the case in an attempt to cool the chip's environment down. Therefore, it also stands to reason that there must be sufficient space for that air to flow. If it was left up to the computer to design itself, computer cases would be larger and with more fans. A little like you might like to live in a larger house with air conditioning, if money was no problem.

Now from the human's point of view. People worry more about looks and fashion and about how much space the computer is taking up. Manufacturers have to pay attention to what people want if they want to sell their computers.

People wanted less prominent computer cases, so producers made half-size cases; people wanted quieter computers, so producers put fewer fans in the cases. And the result was predictable: computers housed in cases like these broke down more often and the only person who was happy about that was the producer.

There is also a trend towards beauty in computer cases. Acrylic, see-through cases are very trendy with gamers. Now games machines are some of the most powerful home computers on the market, because of the power required to run the graphics at a life-like speed.

See-through cases encourage the use of size and fans, because they are often themed, which means that the interior may have green, blue, yellow or red LED's to light it up. So, for instance, when the DVD player kicks in a red LED comes on inside the case. Similarly with fans, which may also be painted. Some of these themed computer cases are perfect for the chips that live in them and the people that own them

Owen Jones

Fighting Off Viruses

Protecting your computer from viruses is becoming more and |more difficult each day. While it may sound a bit paranoid, it is true that you cannot let your guard down for one moment. Even commercial giant Microsoft has found its own systems infected on more than one occasion.

Do you remember the "good old days", before the arrival of the Internet and downloadable programs? Life was straightforward then in terms of computer viruses. The primary way to catch a virus then was via floppy disks. By today's standards, it used to take quite a while before a virus was able to infect a computer and slow down the system.

The antivirus software of that time was usually able to identify and eliminate viruses before they caused too much damage. Moreover, computer users were fairly knowledgeable about how to defend themselves by scanning all floppy disks before using them.

The Internet changed all that. The Internet provided a medium by which viruses could travel from host to host with blinding speed. A computer user had to begin to think about email, email attachments, peer-to-peer file sharing, instant messaging, and software downloads as virus entry points.

Today's viruses can attack through multiple entry points, propagate without human intervention, and take full advantage of weaknesses within a system or program. With technology advancing everyday, and the convergence of computers with other mobile devices, the potential for new kinds of threats also increases.

Luckily, the advancement of antivirus software has kept pace with the virus threats. Antivirus software is essential to a computer's ability to fend off viruses and other malicious programs. These software products are designed to protect against the ability of a virus to enter a computer through email, web browsers, file servers and desktops.

Moreover, these programs offer a control feature that handles deployment, configuration and updating. A computer user should remain diligent and follow a couple of simple steps to guard against the menace of a virus:

You should evaluate your current computer security system. With the danger of a new generation of viruses being able to attack in a large number of ways, the tactic of having just one kind of antivirus software has become obsolete. You have to be sure that you have protected all aspects of your computer system from the desktop to the network, and from the gateway to the server.

Think about a more wide-ranging security system which encompasses several features including antivirus, firewall, content filtering, and intrusion detection. This type of system will make it more difficult for the virus to infiltrate your system.

You should install antivirus software created by a well-known, highly regarded company, because new viruses erupt daily, so it is vital that you update your antivirus software daily. Become familiar with the software's real-time scan feature and configure it to start automatically every time you start up your computer. This will protect your system by automatically checking your computer each time it is powered up.

Set your antivirus software to scan all new programs or files no matter from where they come from and exercise caution when opening binary, Word, or Excel documents of unknown origin especially if they were received during an online chat or as an attachment to an email.

Make sure you perform regular backups in case your system is corrupted. It could be the only way to recover your data if you computer becomes compromised.

There are many applications available to consumers, so with a little research, you should be able to choose the program that is right for you. Many programs provide a trial version which permits you to download the program and test its capabilities.

However, be aware that some anti-virus programs can be difficult to uninstall, so as a precaution make sure you set up a System Restore point and take back-ups before installing it.

What Is Article Marketing

Article marketing is the writing of articles that are pertinent to the subject of the web site that you want to promote. It is useful because the author is permitted to add two hyperlinks to the articles, normally at the bottom, which will allow the reader to click through for further information.

Therefore, if you desired to promote a web site on cookery, you might write a series of articles on styles of cooking or using various kitchen gadgets.

If you send these articles to a general article database, you can assume a pretty low click through rate (CTR), but if you posted it to a cooking blog, you could expect a higher CTR.

The good thing is that everyone who clicks through will know what they are prone to see on your site, so they are focused visitors and focused visitors are more prone to become customers.

The articles that you submit to webmasters of blogs and article databases usually want to check them for length and content, but if you are honest, that is hardly ever a problem Another advantage of article marketing is that these webmasters never shunt your article off their web site when new arrive.

They may put them into archives, but the archives are still readable and scannable by Google and this is an important point as well.

You see, Google rates web sites on their popularity and one of the methods it uses to estimate popularity is how many links there are on the Internet referring back to it. They are called backlinks. People found this out and attempted to work around it (and still do) by swapping back-links.

However, Google rates one-way backlinks higher than mutual links. An article on a blog gives you two one-way backlinks until the blog goes under. If you choose where you post judiciously, this might never happen.

Google also checks to see if the host of your link is relevant to your site, so it is worth posting to sites that are pertinent to yours and Google awards extra merit if the site having your link is an authority site, that is, a top site on that subject.

If you submit an article to an article database and a leading authority site or newsletter on that subject picks it up and prints it, you will get loads of bonus points from Google, shoot up in the ranking, get loads of visitors and more customers.

The message is to write informative, relevant articles and submit them where they can be found. By this I mean, use the largest article databases, because that is where the top people go to look for content if they are stuck and also submit your article to blogs that are relevant to the subject of your article, which should be relevant to the subject of your website, which should be relevant to what you are trying to sell.

I recently had one of my articles picked up. I had 3,450 plus visitors to my web site within two hours and 256 of them became customers. If only it could be achieved every day. The thing is, it can, if you get the strategy right. Stay on target.

Owen Jones

46

Laptop Computer Reviews

Laptop computer reviews are a very important source of information for those who are interested in purchasing a new computer to assist them in their work or to provide entertainment at home. But being an knowledgeable consumer is not an easy job for anybody.

Even though we may consider that we are informed enough, we may later, discover that we were mistaken in the decision we took. Or perhaps that mistake was made in the phase before the decision itself was made? During the research phase maybe?

The rule of thumb is to try and read more than a few laptop computer reviews more before you consider you have gleaned enough information to be able to do what you need. Why is that so important?

To start with, laptop computer reviews are written by people who are paid to write quite a lot of reviews possibly even in one single day. As a result of this, whether the writer wants to or not, he/she may end up saying pretty much the same thing about almost every laptop computer or even just glossing over the details.

Or, she/he may end up leaving sections of information out. Making mistakes is pretty common in human endeavour when exhaustion and boredom enter the picture.

Another reason why you should read as many laptop computer reviews as you can is that this way you will surely come across reviews made by some people who actually use the laptop computer you are interested in. These types of ratings and assessments are the ones that will most probably present you with a down-to-earth picture of how this laptop computer really works.

People who have actually used the computer will also have several points of view that big magazine reviewers may exclude from their pieces or reviews. These types of laptop computer reviews will also give you an idea about whether you are thinking about buying a laptop computer that is best for you or whether you are thinking about buying something that is too advanced for your requirements and so unnecessarily expensive, or too rudimentary, and therefore low-cost but of no use.

Last but not least, different laptop computer reviews, particularly if they come from a number of sites and consumers, will vary in the sort of information they will give you about the laptop computer. What may be absent from one appraisal may be said in another.

The whole mystery will not be over until you actually own that computer. However, the greater the quantity of reviews you read, the more precise the image you will get. Above all, remember that unawareness of the particulars could cost you dearly and more than that, might even land you with a low quality laptop computer.

Owen Jones

Working With Computers

These days most individuals and their grandmothers are using computers on a daily basis to access the Internet and even the so-called computer illiterate operate computers in devices that they have not yet grasped contain them. We are all working with computers all the time whether we comprehend it or not.

Apparatus at work, the car, the mobile telephone and the ATM all have computers built-in to make them more efficient or indeed to make them work at all. Everyone ought to strive to take that small leap to learning how to make use of a computer with a keyboard, especially if they are under fifty.

Not only are we all working with computers, but we are all working with mainframes - the type of computers that NASA uses for its calculations. Where?, you may wonder. Well, when you go to the self-service garage and punch in what you want and how you are going to pay for it, the computer on the petrol pump checks its stock to see whether it can deliver that quantity

Then it tells Head Office that it has supplied that amount and that stock levels have to be decreased by that amount; then it checks you credit card details with the banks' mainframes and then you are free to have your card back and go on your way. And not before. If you do try to escape early, it will already have taken a snapshot of your face and probably your car's registration plate too.

Do you have a security tag to get into work? That will be an RFID (radio frequency ID) tag, which will be communicating with the company's mainframe computer to tell it that 'employee xxx' has turned up for work and it will almost certainly keep tabs on where you are at every other moment of the day too.

Some people used to enjoy doing a little automobile maintenance once a week or once a month (OK, many did not too), but that is now a thing of the past. Before anyone knows what is wrong with a car, they have to plug it in.

Computers

If you go to a main dealer, that knowledge will go into the firm's database to help it design a better car next time (or maybe they will use the data to make certain that it breaks down earlier next time - planned obsolescence).

The purpose here is that if you do not have an idea of what computers can do or indeed are doing, you will be left behind, standing in disbelief in the past wondering what happened to your old life. The easiest manner to find out what computers can do is to start working with computers on a conscious level.

There is just one problem with this article though and that is that because you are reading it on line, I am talking to someone who is already working with computers. Never mind, I tried.

Owen Jones

54

Blogging As An Art Form

If composing is an art form, then blogging can be seen as an art form as well. Blogging is no less an art form than regular writing merely because it is more popularist and does not need paper. Bloggers compose articles on all sorts of items, in fact they write on every subject under the sun. People write about their daily lives, their jobs, their hobbies and their concerns.

Blogging started life in the mid Nineties for webmasters to maintain a record of their involvement with their computers, which is where the term comes from: 'web log'. Web log became weblogs and then it was contracted to blog. Web logs soon became a well-liked manner of recording and publishing other daily activities on line, much like a diary.

Blogs can get posted to a URL like a web site is, or they can be posted to a free bloggers' website. There are many of these free blogs, but one of the most well-known ones is Google's 'Blogger'.

In spite of being free of charge, Blogger offers a fully flexible blog which can hold adverts like Google Ads and Amazon, so that the blogger can offer related items for sale and earn a little money at the same time.

If personal blogs are used to talk on daily life, business blogs can be used as rolling adverts for a firm's products. The manager of the company's blog can write on innovations, new products, jobs vacant and extraordinary offers. The company's blog can be used as a private press release machine which can reach a worldwide audience.

If you want to create a blog for personal or company use, you will have to know something regarding blogging, so here are a few pointers.

This first thing to do is define what your blog is going to be about. If it is a business blog then that is easy, but a personal blog ought to have a target audience. It ought to appeal to a niche group.

Endeavour to keep the niche group quite tight, blogs that waffle on colossal sprawling topics are not as popular.

For instance, stamp collecting is far too wide a subject. Collecting British stamps is better, but British commemorative stamps of the 20th Century is even better. Include some images to keep the blog looking bright and colourful. This is easily done since most contemporary printers have a facility to scan images and send them to your computer.

In the blogosphere, information is the name of the game. Most people surf to gain information. They surf to get the answers to problems that they are undergoing; in order to help with their hobbies or simply for general information. Therefore, you should make your blog a bearer of useful information.

You can make your blog interactive by allowing your readers to leave observations. Some software permits fairly lengthy comments so that visitors can leave their opinions in full. This interactivity will encourage readers to come back to follow the discussion.

In fact, most blogging software will also inform the leaver of a comment that there has been a reply and it will also collect the commentator's email address so that you can add them to a mailing list as long as you supply them with the facility to opt out of the list if they want to.

Internet Marketing Secrets

You are reading this, so it is self-evident that you already do some things on line, but how much do you use the Internet? Do you use it to its full potential? Do you only spend money on the Internet or do you make money on the Net as well?

You might say that you have never spent a penny on line, but that would not be the case, would it? You have a computer that you almost certainly use mostly for going on line and you pay for a broadband connection.

If you find yourself just surfing to use up free time, why not set yourself the aim of using the Net to pay for your monthly connection fees and your next (replacement) computer or a new laptop? That could be a project, a quest, a challenge, if you like.

If you have too much time on your hands this would be a decent excuse to extend your knowledge of computers, the Net and business or business on line too.

If you already have a business, on or off line, you should be using the Internet to advertise it. If you are unfamiliar with the on line ways of promoting, we can stick with traditional off line ways that have been imitated on line.

For example, there are thousands of free on line classified advert web sites. Only type 'free classified ads' into Google and stand back!

However, classifieds are generally perceived as not being as effectual as their off line counterparts. This is because idiots spam these free ads web sites from all over the world merely for a free back link and so many of the ads are irrelevant or not local.

Another form of on line promoting imitated from the 'real world' is banner marketing. Business people can pay to have a banner placed on a relevant web site in order to advertise their firms. It is similar to having a big ad in a newspaper.

Unfortunately, this form of promoting does not work on line so well as it does off line either. Experts say that surfers expect items for free on line, so their eyes 'look through' banner adverts.

So how can you promote your business on line? Well, believe it or not, it by using the very top, up-market off line marketing techniques of having recommendations, reviews and articles written on the items that you are advertising. This would cost thousands or more in a newspaper, but it is virtually free on line.

The number one best way of advertising on line is to compose pieces on or about the issue of your products or firm and posting them to article directories with your URL in the byline. This will give you a back link which Google values very highly in working out your company's ranking in their search engine.

Owen Jones

62

Article Marketing Tips

Many people who create their first web site get a nasty surprise after launching it. They spend a long time thinking about making a website, a long time studying how to build one and a long time creating it. They launch it and wait for visitors to flock to it. And nothing happens. No-one comes by. After a time, they might get four or five visitors and then nothing again.

A lot of individuals reckon that all you have to do is build a web site and it will be indexed by the search engines and then people will find it. This is just not true, although you may become indexed after a time. The problem with this tactic is that when people search on a term and the results appear, there are normally several hundred thousand listings. As an unknown site, yours will be close to the bottom of the heap and most people only look at the first page or two of results.

So, the trick is to get your web site listed on the front page of Google's search returns. Article marketing will help your web site rise in the rankings and become detectable to your potential patrons. It is far better to promote your website so that it will be seen, than to have a showy website that no-one will ever know about. You can add the bells and whistles later, if you still think it is worth while.

The explanation why writing articles works so well at raising your website's visibility, is because of the way that Google operates. Google seeks to rank websites on their popularity, which is supposed to give an indication of its merit. It measures popularity by the number of websites that link back to it. These are called backlinks.

If Google finds a backlink to your website, it checks your website for a reciprocal backlink to the website that holds one to you. Reciprocal backlinks are not as valuable as non-reciprocal backlinks. When you write an article, you are allowed to place two links back to your website (put one to your home page and one to another page).

If you submit that article to an article distribution site (and there are hundreds), other web masters may publish your article with its backlinks. The better the article, the more times it will be published, the more solo backlinks you will get and the higher you will rise in Google. The majority of money made on any search term will be made by the websites at the top of the first page.

There are some other ways of getting back-links, but article promotion is by far the best, steadiest long term tactic for promoting a web site.

Who is likely to publish your article? Well, the distribution website for a start, but also newsletter writers, website owners, bloggers and others who require new content for their own businesses, but who might not have the time or know-how to write their own articles.

Post your article to article directories and websites like MySpace, where they can be found, read and followed back to your website. Perceive the article as a funnel to your website.

Join blogs or produce your own and post them there, but only post pertinent articles on other people's blogs.

When you have a number of related articles, collate them into a book and give it away or sell it with your back-links in situ

Put a link on your website to an autoresponder which will deliver your articles to people who sign up for it.

Some Different Forms Of Affiliate Marketing

There are quite a couple of different types of affiliate marketing. Some of them have become archaic and others have never been so popular. In this article we will be taking a look at some of the better forms of affiliate promoting.

One of the reasons for the on-going popularity of affiliate marketing is that it is inexpensive to set up a web site that could create money. Not just that, but it is possible to earn a few dollars a day without much work and some people have to work twelve hours a day at a hard job for that much. The Net can double their wages on a set-and-forget basis.

Merchants are also keen on affiliate marketing because the structures for implementing affiliate marketing are beneficial to the vendor, because the seller only has to pay a fee on each sale - there is no gratitude for fruitless hard effort.

Having said that, there are methods for the affiliate promoting hopeful to make money, but it necessitates self-discipline. There is a tendency for affiliate marketers to pack as many selling tools - that is, banners - on to every page as they can in the hope that something will please someone.

This is, in fact, the worst approach possible. A web page ought to be targeted. If the campaign is attempting to sell goldfish, that should be the only advert on the page. When the page starts earning money, then you can add adverts for goldfish bowls and goldfish food, but not before.

And certainly do not endeavour to sell 'pet food' in the hope of acquiring at least one sale! There is time for all that later. In the beginning, focus is the watchword. Choose your niche carefully and then have the courage of your convictions to stay with it.

Nowadays there are in essence just two forms of affiliate marketing. They are PPC (pay-per-click) and PPP (pay-per-performance). PPC is very simple to set up and PPP a little more harder, but it can produce higher earnings per click.

PPC is Google's preferred means of promoting, but there are a number of other companies that support PPC as well. Google's Adsense is the biggest network of PPC advertisers. It is very straightforward to set up because it is automatic.

If you want to earn money from PPC, you have to construct a website that is weighty on content - that is, there are useful articles on topics that people would like to find out about. As the web master, you then insert a small piece of code which Google (or one of the other PPC merchants) gives you, and adverts will show up in that location.

Not any old adverts though. The software will scrutinize the surrounding text for keywords and then match them up to keywords that advertisers have bought. The result is that a website that has enabled PPC will have adverts that are relevant to its content and, hopefully, its visitors. If you have a website on tropical fish, then the adverts will be about tropical fish and accessories.

PPP or pay-per-performance is harder to set up only because the web master has to go and find advertisers in the same niche; then ask for an account and then claim their rewards. Having said that, a web master can earn more for one PPP click than a whole days worth of PPC clicks.

PPP can include a number of kinds of actions - the 'performance' part though generally means a sale. Acquiring a sale is much more difficult than procuring someone to check out an offer (PPC). Another benefit of PPP is that you can form a downline.

How To Buy A Computer

As with everything else, purchasing a computer is easy if you know what you are doing. For those who do not know though, it can be a complete nightmare. People who have used a computer before have a good idea about what they require and what they would like, but for those who have never used a computer before, all the components that make up a computer can appear confusing.

The clear answer is to buy the best that you can manage, but this still might puzzle some people, because the best is not always the most expensive. In the computer world, 'the best' usually means the biggest and the fastest.

Just to make it more confusing, 'the biggest' here does not always mean in size, but in capacity. The only large size that is important is the monitor. This is a quick rundown of how to buy a computer and its components:

Before you buy a computer, think about why you want one. If it is for educational reasons: that is surfing the web and looking up content, you do not need more than a basic desktop computer. If you are constantly on the move, then you might need a laptop, or maybe cyber cafes will meet your requirements.

This kind of machine is also sufficient for writing letters and emails and almost any type office work. Top flight computers are only required by games players and exhibitionists.

Buy a complete computer. That means buying a kit of: CPU (the 'computer'), monitor (screen), keyboard, mouse, speakers and printer. This way you will just have to plug everything in and off you go - you can be sure that they are all compatible.

When you purchase your next computer, you can buy all the components individually to get even better value for money or a system more precisely tailored to your preferences.

Go for the largest screen, the fastest memory and fastest hard drive and the biggest memory (RAM) and biggest hard drive (gigabytes) that you can afford. You do not have to have a lot of 'space' for normal office work or normal surfing, but if you get into downloading music or films, then memory soon gets eaten up, although you could always add a new external (plug-in) hard drive later, in need be.

Make sure that you purchase a computer that is not too old, if you go second-hand. This is because you can up-grade computers for two or three years, but after that manufacturers change the casings and new components will no longer fit - planned obsolescence, it is called.

Get your computer from a well-known, trustworthy local store and ensure that it has a good guarantee. Computers do not often go amiss, but you do not want to have to send it half-way across the country and wait three weeks for it to come back. If you are in business, get two. Maybe a laptop and a desktop and synchronize the contents of both so that you always have your data.

Following these guidelines will ensure that the computer novice gets 'enough' of a deal and an adequate machine that is fit for purpose without paying through the nose.

Networking Home Computers

If there are a number of computers in your household, you can easily network them together. Just as if your home were an office. You might be wondering why you should want to do that, but there are good reasons. If business thinks that it is a good concept, then there has to be something to it.

The foremost advantage for a family is the ability to share software. The main advantage for parents is the ability to see what their kids are looking at. Call that spying if you like, I call it taking care. Of course, that is your prerogative, but in an office situation someone is able to observe what traffic passes through the office machines, although in some countries this is illegal or illegal-ish.

The easiest manner to do this is with Ethernet cards or by plugging each computer into a residential gateway, which is often called a router. The Ethernet cards are not costly, but it means running a cable from every computer to the main computer (called a server). This is the fastest and most reliable method.

Otherwise you could plug each computer into the residential gateway using a comparable sort of wire. This latter method has a variation - it can be a wireless connection. However, the wireless connection will mean that all the computers need a wireless card, which means more money and it can be slower and more prone to interception by others outside the house.

There are also more complicated variations on these techniques. For instance, you could link all the upstairs computers by network (also known as LAN) cards and have one of those computers use a wireless connection to the server or router to which the server is connected.

Once the hardware is connected, setting up a local area network (LAN) is not that difficult because Windows has a wizard to help you do it. This is a step-by-step wizard which makes it fairly simple to do, although in practice there are a couple of items that you have to understand to complete the process, not that it should be beyond anyone.

Once up and running, each computer on the LAN will become able to share any file that is designated as 'shared'. The term 'file' includes programs, text, writings, pictures, audio files and anything else on any computer in the house that is designated as 'shared' by its author.

It also means that devices or peripherals can be shared. For instance, you will only have to have one printer and one scanner, which can be shared. Each computer will also be able to take part in multi-player games as well - each in their own rooms in conditions that suit them - lights on or off, et cetera.

Another enormous advantage of having an LAN is the ease of regulating Internet security. It means one firewall, one virus protection system and one anti-spyware system all controlled by the most responsible person in the house or on the LAN.

Owen Jones

78

Spyware, Adware And Computer Viruses

To many computer users spyware, adware and computer viruses are all the same. In a way they are: they have all been sneaked onto your computer and none of them are going to do any good for you, the computer owner. They are all a majestic pain in the neck.

However, there are differences between them and, as a computer owner, you might just as well know what those differences are so that you may correctly decide how much resources you are going to devote to getting shot of them.

Spyware: spyware is like a parasite. It can get delivered to your computer via email attachments, as part of a free program or even as part of a program you paid for. Frequently, spyware is attached to something practical that people pass around because it is useful, funny or pornographic.

When the ebook or email is opened, the parasitic spyware goes off and secretes itself somewhere in your computer. Spyware may do lots of things, but like all decent parasites, it is not there to damage your computer.

It is there to read your key presses, scan your disk drives and record the websites you visit. Then, say, once a week, while the computer is inactive, it sends all this information home to its creator. The creator may then use this knowledge as he or she sees fit, but first they have to untangle it all. Software will do that.

The least that will occur is that the data will show that you have been searching for, say, new shoes on line and you will receive heaps of spam on new shoes. One of the worst things that could happen is that it will have read your banking details and there may be an attempt on your bank account.

Adware: adware is comparable, but it is seen as very nearly legitimate. Typically, a practical program like a download accelerator will record where it has downloaded files for you from and it will report that back to its creator and you will be spammed again.

Theft is not part of the raison d'etre of adware. Look in your cookies and you will see dozens of these little programs collecting information on your each move. Most of the big names in the computer world, including Google, use Adware in the form of cookies to find out what you would like before anyone else can, so that they can be the first to serve it up to you.

Computer Viruses: include Trojans, worms and all the other forms of malware to most people. These are usually disruptive or destructive in nature and intended to ruin your computing or surfing experience. It is simple to understand why someone would create spyware and adware, but not viruses. Some people seem to get a kick out of causing mayhem for others.

The only manner to keep spyware, adware and computer viruses off your computer is by using powerful antivirus software and a firewall. Numerous individuals are pleased with the amount of protection that the free Windows firewall and AV software offers.

Others use the free Windows firewall, but use a third party free AV program. Yet others buy a commercial package that has its own firewall and AV software. It just depends on the degree of protection that you are happy with and whether you are prepared to pay for it.

Playing Old Games On A New Computer

Lots of individuals still like playing the crappy old games of 20-30 years ago. The reason has to be nostalgia because the games of today are more advanced in graphics, speed, playability and sound. Only the content might have deteriorated.

Twenty to thirty years ago, there were cannon games for shooting down planes and blowing up tanks and of course they were being driven by people who got killed, but you never saw them. These days, these same shoot-em ups have blood, gore and body parts scattered everywhere.

Maybe it is more truthful, but does it teach anything? I don't think it makes kids more aware of the horrors of war, it just numbs them to it a little more. In the past, those old cannon games were roughly all about elevating the cannon and permitting for windage, movement and distance. But what is Kitten Cannon about?

There is no skill to the game. You only blast a kitten out of a cannon to its death and the one who shoots it the farthest is the winner. Why a kitten? Only to be gruesome, I imagine. Children like gruesome and the game is addictive and so it is well-liked, but older players are the ones who are looking back to their Super Mario and The Hobbit adventure games.

However, the majority of these old games came on 5.25" floppy, cartridge or cassette tape. A couple were on 2.5" diskettes. However, scarcely anyone has the ability to play these formats any more Some have been converted to run on contemporary PC's, but then you have to buy the same old 20-30 year old game again and the graphics and sound are no better.

You used to be able to play the old games, say, 10-15 years ago by downloading or buying an emulator, because computers back then were (or could) still loading from the old storage devices mentioned previously. So, if you would like to play a boxful of old Commodore 64 or Atari 250 games that you just found in the attic, you will have to try to purchase a 10-15 year old AT or something like that.

The only other option is to hunt the Net for compilation disks that aficionados have put together after copying and converting them for use on contemporary PC's. The newer versions will probably run faster and smoother than what you remember, although the music will still be just as repetitive.

It is up to you what you think about copyright law. I am pretty certain that most of the firms that made most of those games no longer exist, but it is probable that someone still owns the copyright although they may no longer care whether it is infringed so long as you do not attempt to sell hundreds of disks of the games on eBay.

Maybe the old games of 20-30 years ago were far happier than the contemporary variety. Computers were still new and exciting in the Eighties and Nineties and I don't remember any blood and guts being shown in any of the games and I don't think anyone considered firing a kitten out of a cannon.

Owen Jones

86

PCmover by Laplink

A fortnight ago, I ordered a new laptop, something that I tend to do roughly every four or five years. I liken it to moving into or even buying a new house. There is a sense of excitement at the increased speed and enhanced features, but also of dread because of having to move all my stuff or files.

The last time I rehoused all my data was between two Asus laptops. There was a Microsoft utility that came with the devices making it extremely easy, if a little time-consuming, to transfer my data. I had to connect the two computers with a serial cable, click a couple of buttons, and seventeen hours later, the job was done.

Perfectly!

So, when my new computer arrived, the first thing I did was look for the file transfer utility.

No utility!

So, I did a search of Google for "transfer files between two computers".
The news was that MS had discontinued it, but that it had partnered with a firm called Laplink, that produced an exact same app called Pcmover.

Alarm bells went off in my head but I didn't know why.

Why would a successful company want to ditch a successful product?

Well, the answer is that the free version of PCmover is practically useless, because it doesn't transfer apps and settings... or doesn't transfer settings anyway.

What use is that?

If you want to move the whole shebang over, it costs $20.

How mean can a multi-billionaire get, eh?

I can afford $20, but I live in Asia and I know that a laptop costs most buyers four to five months gross wages. Most Asians don't have a credit card either, so they get their new device home, only to find out that cheapo Bill Gates had condemned them to several days of transferring files manually.

Anyway, so I swallowed my disgust and bought the upgrade, but couldn't find out how to use it to transfer files (content) over my network, even with my forty years of IT experience. I contacted the support help line and a fantastic guy called Jefferson took over my computers by remote control and effected the data transfer.

It was only the next day that I realised that all of my personal login data, all of my browsers and half of my applications were missing - they had not been transferred. Thunderbird, my email client, was left behind too and when I re-installed it, I lost all my contacts! Using PCmover by Laplink has caused my biggest computer disaster for twenty years!

So, I have spent the last three days manually copying files between my laptops. Looking up log-in details and re-registering apps to transfer data correctly is tedious, time-consuming work.

Owen Jones

Do not use Laplink's PCmover, it is a piece of junk, and do not trust MS or its founder – I never will again.

Contact Details

Facebook: AngunJones
Twitter: @owen_author
Blog: Megan Publishing Services
Amazon Author's Page: Owen Jones on Amazon

This book is part of the 'How to...' series of 125 manuals by Owen Jones.
The whole series can be found in many languages on Megan Publishing Services at:
https://meganthemisconception.com